Wha's Like Us?

on the Unrealities of Being Scottish

Andrew Burnside

ARGYLL✠PUBLISHING

© Andrew Burnside

First published 2007
Argyll Publishing
Glendaruel
Argyll PA22 3AE
Scotland
www.argyllpublishing.com

The author asserts his moral rights.

**British Library Cataloguing-in-Publication Data.
A catalogue record for this book is available from
the British Library.**

ISBN 978 1 906134 08 2

Printing: Mackays of Chatham

We are what we pretend to be, so we should be careful about what we pretend to be.

Kurt Vonnegut

Contents

Prologue

Nikos Dimou wrote *The Misfortune of Being Greek* in 1975, during the time of the military government. Since then there have been many reprints. The book consists of 192 observations on his fellow Greeks, their attitudes and perceptions. Observation number 19 is:

> The premise of this book is that contemporary Greeks, because of their history, their inheritance, and their character, experience a broader divide between their desires and reality than does the average man.

Well, now, could Greek actually compete with Scot in this matter of 'divide'? A copy of the book had to be got.

A start was made on Scottish observations with only a general impression of the Greek original. At first the idea of flyting – from the time of Dunbar and the Stewart court – appealed. But the problem with flyting is that the hurling of abuse as vicious and slanderous as possible was its one and only purpose. Such was not mine; rather it was to make accurate, if pointed, observations on Scotland and the Scot.

Since putting these observations together, I have had a go at Dimou's book armed with dictionary and grammar. There happens, I believe, to be much in common between both sets of observations but the differences, I think, are also great (and just as well, or we would not be Scots). For Dimou the unhappiness of the modern Greek is due to the split between his desires and his reality. The Scot, on the other hand, has more than others built – and goes on building – a divide between reality and what he imagines he is; but the Scot, as a Scot, does not show desire for much – and happiness doesn't rate high.

Revisiting *Misfortune* after many years, Dimou wrote:

> I have tried, simply, to articulate my observations in such a way that serious people

will find them serious, while the less serious
will find them less serious. I am now tortured
by the thought that the exact opposite might
happen.

What hope, then, for these Scottish observations? Greece has had independence for almost two
hundred years since throwing off the Turkish yoke.
Scotland has 'enjoyed' its new non-independent
Parliament (since being 'given' it) for no time at all
and is not sure what yoke it was, or is, under.

'Serious' people in Scotland like to reject anything said that is not totally Pangloss about Scotland. As for the others (that is, almost all), who flit
between extremes of self-denigration and ego-
inflation, perhaps these observations will be broad
enough for them to address their unrealities. Our
myths do not exist independently, but as a mutually
supporting whole. Knocking off one at a time won't
do; but, if liberated from the whole enthistlement,
might not the Scot see clearly and act with energy?

'Wha's Like Us. . . ?'

1 Education

We're the best; a lack of Nobel prizes proves nothing.

2 Health

We're world-beaters. For years we have successfully defended our lead in death rates from cancer and heart disease. Lately, too, we've forged ahead in asthma.

3 History

We don't need others' lessons. Don't need, e.g. the holocaust – we had the Highland Clearances. Don't need the French revolution – we have Burns.

4 Geography

We're not really interested in other countries: of other peoples, our concern is to be certain that we're better; of other lands, that ours is fairer.

5 Industrial Revolution

We started it; we invented everything it needed.

6 Future

The world becomes more homogeneous. The Scot, however, cannot imagine that he and Scotland will be other than he imagined he and it were.

7 Self-image

> *'Scotland, the best small country in the world.'*
> (Jack McConnell, Scotland's First
> Minister, G8 Gleneagles, July 2005)

> 'Scotland **small**?
> Our multiform, our infinite, Scotland **small**?'
> (Hugh MacDiarmid)

8 '. . . Damn few, an' they're a' deid!'

Aggrandisement, self put-down, in one.

Auld Lang S(Z)yne

9 Scotland's past is full of golden eras in whose glow
we bask continuously.

10 The present is not a golden era – all such are past.
In the future, the present may be considered a
golden era.

11 Scotland's past is full of disappointments, defeats
and disasters in whose gloom we lurk
continuously.

12 The Scot's sense of reality – insofar as he has one
– comes through the gloom of disappointments,
defeats and disasters which blind him to all else.

13 The Scot's sense of reality – insofar as he has one
– comes through the soft-tint of past splendours
which blind him to all else.

14 As creation myths to religion, so Wallace and
Bruce to Scottish national identity; incapable of
being viewed rationally or of being ditched.

15 The Scot's psyche is massively influenced by tales of wee, local skirmishes long, long ago. National psyches need an occasional spring-clean; one for Scotland – and a big one! – is long overdue.

16 The Scot, locked up in his chosen delusional past, cannot imagine a future.

Kitsch

17 We – i.e. Sir Walter Scott – were world firsts in kitsch; Queen Victoria gave it Royal approval; now we're scarcely more than this institutionalised nonsense and, tartan-branded, are hooked on the cash it attracts.

18 'Braveheart' – screenplay by Sir W. Scott. Yes, if he was around!

19 Lowlanders achieved their historic goal of ethnically cleansing the Gaels by using them as extras in their new, tartanised, non-nation.

20 Scottish Tartan Week (New York, Spring each
   year) carries kitsch to ever greater lows. It attracts
   people who lack taste and judgement – that is,
   visiting Scottish politicians and many Americans.

21 As the British Army needs fewer troops, pipe
   bands (invented by the British Army to march
   Jock to war) are left to play at Highland Games
   (patronised by British Royalty to amuse and
   legitimise British Royalty).

22 'Scots Wha Hae', 'Scotland the Brave', 'Flower of
   Scotland' – three huge steps in the onward, and
   ever downward, march of kitsch.

23 More Lowlanders than Highlanders suffered from land clearance; no one 'celebrates' this; it's not part of our chosen, kilted, kitsch, self-image.

24 Kitsch – the essence of Scottish culture – defined by a foreign word.

25 Kailyaird – kitsch, only less stylish (it's the home consumption variety).

26 *'Gaelyaird'* – as in *'Granny's hielan hame'* – Kailyaird for a lost, Gaelic hovel invented by, and expressed in, Lowland Scots.

Character

27 All peoples need a flattering self-image, small ones most of all. Scots invest so much in maintaining theirs that they've little energy left for anything else.

28 Continual failure by states, as by people, creates a victim mentality. Scots, as Scots, have this. Lose it and they'll lose their historic identity.

29 Lack of initiative – a critical survival strategy for the Scot at home. It equips him to endure familiar failings, helps him avoid the criticism of getting above himself, and avoids the risk of major failure had he aspired.

30 Abroad, the Scot is traditionally famed as
thrusting, optimistic and entrepreneurial – the
quality so well conserved at home by underuse.

31 The Scot imagines he's a world beater;
occasionally he gets glimpses of how far he falls
short of that; so he returns to the comfort blanket
of myth.

32 Burns voiced our fundamental and deep-rooted
belief in fairness and in the nobility of the
common man. Had he in fact gone to slave
plantations in the West Indies, we would have
heard a lot less of this fundamental and deep-
rooted belief and its companion – the notion that
you don't have to do anything to be as good as
anyone

33 The Scot is born free. He has his own law,
religion and education. Law is more and more
constrained internationally; few profess religion;
education grows less distinct between countries.
The Scot is born free.

34 The Scot is not free. He is hooked on outworn
myths and illusions – the adult equivalents of
baby's dummy.

35 Scots have given the world a song that expresses
the very essence of their being – 'Auld Lang Syne'.
It is sung on every occasion that calls for the
soggy, the sentimental and the bogus – the very
essence of their being.

36 Scots – a hard-headed, logical, people unable to drop negative habits; imaginative care, not a sermon, is needed to make them positive.

37 Scots – a people with a fine, subtle, sense of humour – not in evidence when the jokes are about their country and by Englishmen.

38 Where once there was popular religious zeal and collective struggle, now there is only private apathy. As ever, the Scot takes things to the extreme.

39 Scots love losers: e.g. William Wallace, Bonnie Prince Charlie, William McGonnagal, Jimmy Maxton, Tommy Sheridan. Tommy's Scottish Socialists wanted shipbuilding to return to the Clyde. Forget the hardships: work – deafness from riveting, lung disease from asbestos, etc; or home – drink, poverty, abuse, etc. How we love, and always will, our lovely losers, our true bearers of national charisma.

40 Two 'musts' to become a famous Scot: live abroad; have fame conferred by non-Scots.

41 Harry Lauder's joke about the mean Scot allowed the English to laugh at, not fear, the Scot; it also let Lauder laugh his way to the bank.

42 Scots have a keen sense of justice – correction – injustice.

43 Few in Scotland are of ethnic origin; that's why we're so non-racist.

Society

44 If no one is more than six personal contacts from anyone else on earth, in a small place like Scotland it's two or less. It's handy for bringing people together, but in such as politics, the media, the arts, law, medicine, etc, it means nobody speaks out about anything.

45 *'Kent his faither'* – the put-down for anyone who steps out of – that is, up from – the tribe into which he was born.

46 Small, enclosed, communities can be a living hell. Scotland comprises many, small, enclosed, communities.

47 The feudal lord required the support – yea, admiration – of his vassals. Absentee Highland landlords (Royal, Arab, Billy Connelly) still crave admiration as chieftain at some wee, pretendy, Highland Games.

48 With the demise of clan chiefs and loss of status of teachers, doctors and ministers, who can Scots look up to? Not the wee, pretendy, Parliament!

49 The spirit of clan loyalty (lifetime obeisance to the chief) lived on for generations among officials in local authorities – leaving them beholden to the every whim of their small-town, small-minded, unemployed, politico-careerist masters.

50 Visitors adore Scottish accents – even if some are less than lilting. To the Scot, accent is as urine spray to the dog – an instant source of all he needs to know about his fellow creature.

51 Most Scots speak English **and** a local patois; tribal pressures mean many choose not to set aside the patois when speaking to someone not of the tribe.

52 After the Union with England of 1707, aspiring Scots strove to speak less like Scots; this continues; it supports a profitable fee-paying school-industry and divides the nation.

53 Gaelic survives in the north west of Scotland less for its poetic qualities as for its convenience to locals talking about visitors behind their backs.

54 The Scottish establishment doesn't exist – except as an ape-English, leftish-corporatist, oil-and-water mix which compensates for its smallness and poverty of thought by a hugely puffed-up self-regard.

55 The Scottish anti-establishment doesn't exist – couldn't exist. A critic in Scotland is one who's not in the would-be establishment – yet! All the rest are collaborators with the Scottish establishment (as above).

56 We can't imagine or enable an anti-establishment;
we've whined so long about things; it would be
too painful to break the habit.

57 Scotland has never had a strong, financially and
intellectually independent sector. Its rich were/are
pre-occupied with holding onto wealth and
position; its poor with survival and (nowadays)
obtaining state handouts. In between, it's just
public salariat, small town traders, big town
accountants –all programmed to kiss the hand
that feeds.

58 The new devolved administration starkly exposes
that administration but, even more, the lack of a
strong, creative, secular, non-government, sector.

59 Any critique that might come from academics is
   silenced by short tenure and the need to toe the
   line (alias state 'targets') to secure funds.

60 Scots explored the world to bring it the benefit of
   their knowledge and to study exotic customs.
   Time for fresh exploration and study – an
   anthropological one of ourselves and our own
   myths and customs.

Fighting

61 We have the beating of anyone, anywhere,
anytime. Hard-headed realists, us.

62 Scots, once 'bonny fechters', have now – through
diligent practice – developed a splendid line in
being 'bonny losers'.

63 Our victory celebrations are huge in intensity;
the inverse of frequency.

64 The pipe band was invented by the British Army
to march off Lowlanders dressed as Highlanders
to fight for Britain with Scottish pride.

65 Many think the young urban Scot's dedication to drinking – especially on Saturdays – gets him into fighting afterwards. Wrong! His dedication is to fighting – he just fits in some preliminary drinking, especially on Saturdays.

66 Scotland should seek reparation from Britain. Encouraged to fight for the Empire, urban Scots have evolved to fight but are now denied adequate career opportunities.

67 'There was a soldier, a Scottish soldier –' maudlin sentiment about some golden past – that is, when Scots hacked and shot on behalf of the Auld Enemy.

68 Long ago Scots fought in armies across Europe. The many pale-faced, red-haired, people found across Europe may not be entirely due to this.

Drink

69 The Scot drinks more than most. Not so much because of genes as 'culture'. Long drinking sessions – with a wide mix of alcohols (a *'hauf an' a hauf'*) – hardens his system to inebriation – and everything else.

70 'A good night out' for the young urban Scottish male is: getting out of his skull, vomiting vindaloo on the street, and being incapable of work next day. Truly epic is the language and lifestyle of the young urban Scot.

71 'Drink is the curse of the working class'. This couldn't have come from a Scotsman. For that, 'drink' and 'work' would need to be interchanged.

72 *'Freedom and whisky gang thegither'*. Burns
   confused freedom with licence. His countrymen
   now maintain this as a tradition!

73 Whisky and arguing gang thegither, more like it.
   The cratur frees Scots logic from the normal
   requirements of balance and reasonableness.

74 'No bad' – as enthusiastic as the Scot can be.
   Slow, quiet, drinking intensifies this state. Quick,
   excessive, drinking transports him to ecstasy, rage
   or despair; whatever, it dependably ensures that
   he avoids happiness.
   (Dr Johnson, *'Come, let me know what it is that
   makes a Scotchman happy!'* apparently said when
   ordering for **himself** [sic!] a glass of whisky.)

75 Scots overflow with sentimentality for wee, small, things; it's the nearest they have to feelings: and it goes down just great with drink.

76 All men are born with a deep, existential hunger – whether for things material or spiritual. So, too, the Scot – except his hunger takes a purely liquid form.

77 Single malt Scotch whisky; Scotland's truest cultural achievement; with it, the Scot can get drunk with a 'wee bit of class.'

78 *'Tam lo'ed him like a verra brither.*
   They had been fou for weeks thegither.'
   Main form of love shown by Scotsmen – man-to-man, drunken, fruitless.

79 Scots drink to forget. What they're trying to forget, they've forgotten. It's unlikely that they'll ever remember what they forgot, but certain that they'll never forget to drink to its memory.

Sex

80 Mary Queen of Scots – our only world-famous
   Scotswoman; she was easy on the eye, a big loser,
   and wasn't a real Scot. Flora MacDonald? What
   sane person would have chosen to take drunken
   Charlie over a duck-pond, let alone the open sea?
   Jean Armour? Clarinda? – Bard's Bauds!

81 Centuries ago, the Stone of Destiny was taken to
   Westminster Abbey. It came back recently.
   Centuries ago, Mary Queen of Scots' bones were
   taken to Westminster Abbey. There they remain!

82 *'She was still a virgin at seventeen –*
   A remarkable thing in Aiberdeen.'
                    Male optimism, North-East variety

83 Granny – Scotland's favourite pin-up. Old, and soon to be a memory, she fits sentimentality to perfection.

84 Wearing the kilt should be compulsory. This, and a ban on wearing anything under it, would keep sperm cool and halt population decline.

85 The kilt was highly functional for Scottish soldiers – handy both for fornication and diarrhoea. Nowadays trendy club-goers wear it.

Education and language

86 We began a national education system as early as the sixteenth century; axiomatically, therefore, our education system's the best.

87 Our embarrassment at our education attainment is less that we are so poor at foreign languages as that the use of our own is so poor that English-speaking visitors cannot understand us.

88 The *'lad o' pairts'* – the old, fond example of the humble pupil's desire to learn and the dominie's commitment to teach. Of zero relevance today!

89 Scots have immense pride in their education
   system; Scots who can afford the fees send their
   children to schools that offer A-levels.

90 *'A guid Scots tongue in his heid'*. We're so educated
   and articulate! Few others would understand this
   tongue, even if the Scot untied it.

91 It takes a pretty downbeat education system and
   language to create a negative out of two positives –
   Aye, Right!

92 Small is good; small **and** old **and** pathetic really
   turns us on – as in 'a little, wee, bit, wifiekin'.
   Smallness in five-dimensions.

93 As Scots need to be **Not** English, they need a
Not-English language – 'Scots'. This was fine for a
parochial, eighteenth century, rural, mindset;
but. . .

94 The Scottish diminutive of awful is *'awfy'*; that's
condemnation plus affection; total opposites;
four letters.

95 *'Wee'* denotes: (1) affection for; (2) contempt for –
'wee, pretendy, Parliament'; and (3) negation and
affection – 'wee bastard'; total opposites (and
more); three letters

Economy

96 Scotland is (a) naturally poor; (b) naturally rich.
(a) Dr Johnson *'the noblest prospect which a
Scotchman ever sees is the high road to England!'*
(b) Sir David Lindsay *'So laik we no thing that to
nature nedis.'*

97 The Scottish economy is: a Celtic tiger awaiting
independence; a not-doing-so badly part of the
UK economy that might just do worse by itself.

98 The Scottish Economy – (i) a hypothetical
concept, ever more so as globalisation proceeds;
(ii) a major industry, employing droves of
academic economists.

99 Scotland's main economic burden is not its wrinklies, but its schemies – its post-industrial, non-proletariat, subsidyites.

100 Not as rich as the Lanarkshire coalfields in their day, but seams of genealogical records are being profitably mined in Scotland thanks to those who left. More emigration's needed to sustain this industry in future!

101 Scottish entrepreneurs: we're not sure about them. Are they successes worthy of emulation or just exploiting us? Anyway, there are so few of them, a proper opinion cannot yet be formed.

102 Our natural economic endowment: **positive**: land, wind, rain; **negative**: land, wind, rain.

103 We are an English-speaking country; this should be an economic advantage; except, few others can understand us.

104 Our three economic epochs: pre-industrial; industrial; and post-industrial. We love the first two because they've been and gone. We are unable to address the third because it's here and now.

105 Our time of economic success (i.e. manufacturing) was due to: (1) a 'Klondyke'; (2) technological advance; (3 and mainly) Imperial Preference. (1) might recur!

106 We're stuck with tourism as a major industry. Happily, there's a limit to those who want to hear bagpipes – ah, but, the Chinese haven't arrived yet!

The English

107 If the English did **not** exist it would be
necessary to invent them so that the Scot could go
on **not** being himself.

108 If England did **not** exist, it would **not** have been
necessary for Scotland to invent itself as it is; if
Scotland did **not** exist, England would be much
the same; this asymmetry hurts the Scots' sense of
importance.

109 The Scot is always examining his past,
convinced there must be something within it **not**
yet discovered which would, beyond doubt,
establish his pre-eminence over the whole world –
well, England anyway.

110 Scotland is a small country that acts as big as England and knows it's **not**.

111 We do **not** have the conviction to do anything for its own sake. Conviction arises only when the doing demonstrates to ourselves (no one else gives a damn) that we're **not**-English.

112 In England, the *nouveaux riches* are looked down upon by their betters for a lack of breeding. **Not** so in Scotland; here the *anciennes pauvres* despise them – for having escaped the clutches of the tribe (*'Kent his faither'*).

113 Scotland has one victory per millennium against the English (on battle or sports field); **not** being optimistic is a necessary survival adaptation.

114 If a Scot celebrated England's **not** winning at sport, it would be because he did **not** have much opportunity to celebrate Scotland's success.

115 Scotland had twice the share of men in the British army as it had of the British population. Scots admit **no** blame for the excesses of the British Empire. We blame the English – as (very decently!) does all the world.

116 If Scotland had **not** had to fight England so much, it would have had more time for its other hobbies – e.g. internal civil or religious feuding.

117 Scotland had twice the share of men in the British army as it had of the British population; war dead, war loss, **not** less.

118 London is described as **neither** English **nor** British, just a place where people live because it pays them to be there. Scotland is Scottish because it's a place where it does **not** pay its people to be.

119 England – a **not** so small, **not** so far away country, about whom we do **not** know much.

120 Scots are **Not**-English.

121 If Dr Johnson had **not** declared that the fairest prospect a Scotchman could behold was the highway to England, we would all have taken it.

122 Displays of a country's nationalism do **not** appeal much to others; to the Scot, displays of English nationalism do **not** have any appeal at all.

Culture

123 We are on the edge of the civilised world; culture gets here late. If we'd had it longer and if it covered our post-glacial landscape better, we might not think that every piddling-little artistic effort of ours was a world shattering event.

124 Culture fascinates us as a strange, exotic, thing. We feel it's good for us, we taste it in small quantities. It does have positive effects, but only in strict proportion to intake.

125 Our problem is not so much with what Burns, MacDiarmid, etc, wrote, but that, as it's such a small corpus, it falls woefully short of forming a national culture. Thus our traditions nurture and crush us simultaneously.

126 Ban *'Flower of Scotland'* – total claptrap. Edward can't be sent home or think again. Let the Scot think ('think again' even – if he's tried it before).

127 Cultural dysfunction (1) Scottish culture is enjoyed by ordinary people who don't like the 'real' stuff. They keep genuine Scottish culture alive within a kitsch, sentimental, saccharine, folksiness.

128 Cultural dysfunction (2) 'real' culture comes from far away and is appreciated by our better sorts. (Only a foreigner could have been entrusted with the design of the Scottish Parliament.)

129 It might have been helpful to our cultural self-esteem if Cumbernauld town centre had been designed by a foreigner, not the new town corporation.

130 It might yet prove helpful to our cultural self-esteem that the new Scottish Parliament has indeed been designed by a foreigner.

131 Scottish culture is for the ordinary people. It gives the upper classes, aping English speech and manners, the cringe. Culture divides.

132 Question for the cultured Scot – what is the nationality of the poet who wrote a cycle of twenty sonnets to Mary Queen of Scots? Hint: it's one of English, French, German, Italian, Russian, or Scottish.

133 Bad as they were, the Highland Clearances should be a cause of great rejoicing – for creating a diaspora to save Gaelic culture at risk of extinction in its native land.

134 Faery Queen, return to the Eildons! Capture, then free, a new Thomas the Rhymer. One Scot might then see clearly and speak the truth.

135 Scots at international sporting competitions
   paint their faces blue. The Picts did much the
   same in battle. So much for cultural progress. So
   much, too, for the lessons of history – the Picts
   also got a gubbing.

136 *'Whisky and freedom gang thegither'*- and **him**
   gathering excise duty!

137 We must be so grateful that Burns never wrote
   about midges. If he had, we'd be plagued by his
   verses even more than by the brutes themselves.

138 Auld Lang Syne – nostalgia for great resistance of long ago – regret for tragic or unjust loss. Burns didn't invent all this, but his verse ensures they're right at the heart of the modern Scottish myth.

139 MacDiarmid listed Anglophobia as a hobby. Really he had – and Scots have – much better things to do.

140 The three main Scottish musical tempi are: manic; smaltzy (waltzy) or keening. An accurate representation of the national psyche.

141 Lots of Scots went abroad over the centuries;
some returned; despite this, Scotland's general
level of civilisation remains low.

142 Whatever the Scottish Culture Commission may
say, expect from our politicians nothing except
Young Urban Community Kitsch – **YUCK**.

The Caledonian Anti-Syzygy

143 The Scot suffers a double whammy: the
conviction that he's superior to, and more
distinguished than, all others; and the conviction
that he's inferior to, and less distinguished than,
all others.

144 We won't change. We're satisfied being
dissatisfied with ourselves.

145 We love argument; it intoxicates us; and, as with
alcohol, when intoxicated we abandon all sense of
proportion. (*'Tam tint his reason a' thegither.'*)

146 Most Scots think they would like to live in a
romantic village in the Highlands if it were near:
a supermarket, a multiplex cinema, a range of
good shops; and had a good climate and an
international airport. Scots do not in general
choose to live where they think they would like to
live.

147 Dunoon, a small, sleepy, ageing, town on the west
coast of Scotland boasts – with not a trace of irony
- the motto 'Forward'. It is Scotland writ small.

148 Many Scots loathe their own country so much that they go and live in another one and establish Caledonian Societies.

149 Urban Scotland is divided between Glasgow and Edinburgh – an inevitable result of anti-syzygy – nothing exists between them (except, Falkirk).

150 MacDiarmid's phrase.* Absolutely wrong about everything, he was right on this. These present observations are in large part variations on this theme. (Which is why they're placed right in the middle!)

---

*The term Caledonian Antisyzygy was not first coined by MacDiarmid but by G. Gregory Smith in his 1919 book Scottish Literature: Character and Influence:

> the literature of Scotland is the literature of a small country. . . it runs a shorter course than others. . . we find. . . that cohesion. . . is only apparent, that

the literature is remarkably varied, and that it
becomes, under the stress of foreign influence,
almost a zigzag of contradictions. . . . Perhaps in
the very combination of opposites – 'the Caledonian antisyzygy' – we have a reflection of the
contrasts which the Scot shows at every turn, in his
political and ecclesiastical history, in his polemical
restlessness, in his adaptability. . . Oxymoron was
ever the bravest figure, and we must not forget that
disorderly order is order after all.

MacDiarmid developed the whole idea in 'The Caledonian
Antisyzygy and the Gaelic Idea' published in *The Modern
Scot* 1931-2. But he was on to it, in principle anyway,
before that, e.g. in 'A Drunk Man Looks at the Thistle' 1926:

On the Unrealities of Being Scottish

I'll ha'e nae hauf-way hoose, but aye be whaur
Extremes meet – it's the only way I ken
To dodge the curst conceit o' bein' richt
That damns the vast majority o' men.

And so, the Caledonian antisyzygy headed off to where it is
nowadays, way beyond the bounds of literary/intellectual
matters, off to things as seeingly remote as 'aa fur coat and
nae knickers', the delicate image of our capital city.
For some, like MacDiarmid, the duality in the Scottish soul
suggested a creative tension. Others were less sure that
extremes might meet. In *Stone Voices*, Neal Ascerson
summed up the contradictions of the Scottish national
character as: 'The St Andrew's Fault; the deep geological
fault running underneath national self-confidence.'

Fitba'*/Religion

(or anything vaguely passionate)

151 We invented football; we're naturals at it; we've just had a bad run for the last 100 years or more.

152 The manager of the Scotland squad commands immense public regard. He should be given full presidential powers.

153 When English soccer* fans were sober and well-behaved, Scots fans were poisonous dwarves. When English fans became yobs, the Scots became fun, party-people in kilts – i.e. **Not-English**.

---

* Fitba' = football (around the world, not just Scotland) = soccer (but only in England and America, where 'football' is a term used for games where the ball is largely propelled by hand)

154 Scottish football's greatest year was 1967. **Not just** because we beat England in England when England were World Champions, but because Jim Baxter played 'keepie-uppie' and did **not** try to score again. A real Scottish achievement – hollow. The video recording remains a best-seller to this day.

155 Ban fitba; illegal status might just ensure a decent standard was attained.

156 Our ancestors went abroad to fight as mercenaries. Ban fitba' here and our boys (pipes and kilts, etc) can find good work supporting other nations.

157 The English take defeat at soccer awfy seriously,
   having had a bit of success from time to time.
   Business opportunity for defeat-rich Scots:
   counselling English fans, grief-stricken after the
   latest 'unlucky' loss.

158 Scotland was once a world beater at 'its' games –
   football, 7-a-side rugby, golf, curling, etc. We need
   something new – to be the best for a while. (Good
   news here: Scots in Nepal became the first ever
   world champions at elephant polo!)

159 *'Win or lose, geht on the booze'* The tartan army's
   anthem – and a damn sight better than the kitsch
   stuff belted out officially.

160 The Calvinist Scot brooked no hierarchy
between himself and God. He didn't need to kow-
tow to any religious hierarchy; he already touched
the forelock at every possible opportunity to every
other conceivable authority.

161 If God did not exist, Rangers and Celtic would
have had to invent him.

162 Few Scots profess any religion. If they do, it's to
distinguish themselves from others who have (or
who they believe may have) a religious affiliation
other than their own (if they really had one).

163 Bill Shankly:

> *'Football isn't a matter of life or death –*
> *it's more important than that.'*

Good joke. Pity is, Scots take it as gospel.

164 Beware fundamentalists, especially Scots who put all their faith in fitba'.

165 Golf – quintessential game of the Scot. In it, you struggle against yourself forever and never quite win.

166 For two years, John Knox felt the lash on the
benches of French galleys. After the Reformation,
parishioners got a lifetime of the same on his
pews.

167 Calvinism – now dead as a creed in Scotland –
has left the Scot with a sense of sin; not the sin of
the Catholic – to be removed by confession; but a
bleak, fatalistic, unburdenable, sin where even a
glimmer of happiness is a matter of guilt,
something 'to be paid for'.

168 Calvinism – origin of the divorce between Scots'
head and heart.

169 *'Why are we so geuoood?'* – the chant of Scots fans when their team is losing 4:0 to some unknown, 'rubbish', foreign outfit.

170 *'We wis robbed!'* – classic expression of Scottish football fan objectivity in the face of loss. Widely used in politics also.

171 Scotland has no sites where God has revealed himself; a tribute both to the nature of the Scot and God's wisdom.

172 Scotland should help immigrants set up football teams – e.g. one for Hindus, Moslems, etc, as for the Irish long ago. We might one day, thereby, have at least six (instead of just four) decent teams and the SPL could be replaced by a small elite: the SSL – Scottish Sectarian League.

173 Racial integration of Muslims will be complete when Sunnis and Shias enjoy street fights in Glasgow. (*'See you, Sunni, yer a right, wee, Shiite.'*)

174 Moslem Fundamentalism here would restore one of our golden eras – when we revelled in religious (albeit Christian) bigotry and martyrdom.

175 Scots applaud Italy when they beat the Scottish
XV; the Scots' history of loss encourages
empathy; anyway they hope to beat Italy some
time soon.

176 Worse than the Scottish XV losing to England is
the English press rubbishing the Scottish XV
when they have just beaten England.

177 Orangemen show little intolerance of Moslems,
Hindus, etc. This is a benign effect (and the only
one!) of their hatred of F***ing Papes.

178 Orangeman – an extreme sort of Scot: mired in a
self-created myth of no advantage to him
whatsoever.

179 Orangemen: common in the West of Scotland; more so in Ulster. They fear Ulster's integration within Ireland. Eh!? Why should Ireland want such crazy fundamentalists stuck in a time-warp of their own creation?

Environment

180 Scotland's climate is not very hot, cold, dry or wet. Its temperate nature contrasts with that of its population.

181 Our climate is changeable; we remain stubbornly the same.

182 Scotch Mist: a fine, dense, drizzle; less thick than Scots Myths.

183 A spell of fine weather (i.e. two days) makes the Scot feel guilty or fearful; he responds with *'We'll pay for this'*; come Global Warming, it'll be *'We're paying for it now!'* – intoned with a deep satisfaction.

184 Tourists love our 'natural wilderness'. Aye, right! – it's all about over-grazing and de-forestation, Lowland tools to ethnically cleanse the Gael.

185 His native forests felled; the Scot now tells others to preserve theirs.

186 Scots love 'their' natural wilderness. Aye, right! Theirs it isn't, theirs it wasn't, theirs it'll never be (apart from a few wee islands). It's the property of a few, absentee, landlords who like to play at being wee, pretendy, lairds.

187 Much of Scotland's geology is pre-Cambrian. We are stubborn and unchanging – even at bedrock.

188 We preserve historic buildings just as they've
   fallen, as if our history had reached an end – our
   landscape (like our minds) littered with ruins.

189 If Global Warming halts the Gulf Stream, a new
   Ice Age may cover Scotland. So, hell might very
   well freeze over at last!

190 Scotland's national parks are designed to bring
   in people to areas of fragile, natural, beauty – and
   destroy it; unless, that is, they get more cash to
   protect that beauty – and bring in yet more people
   to justify the cash, etc, etc.

191 Our first National Park – a pander to mass-
   tourism; 'Lomond Shores' – urban car park,
   urban shopping mall. *'Tak the low road!'*

Scottish Tourism

192 Visitors know Scotland is beautiful; they've seen
the postcards.

193 Visitors appreciate Scotland's scenery. Just as
well for them! At 1-55 of a summer afternoon
they're at least able to feast on the view.

194 We love foreign visitors. Their desire for the full
tourist experience is almost equal to our love of
talking about who we choose to think we are.

195 We love foreign visitors because we can't stand
our fellow countrymen.

196 William Wallace has a simple monument at his presumed birthplace, and a huge, nineteenth century pile near Stirling. The latter is much visited, especially by Americans. In tourism, authenticity is all!

197 Nessie, the world's most effective marketing idea, came into 'existence' before VisitScotland; which was lucky for it, as it would never have happened after VisitScotland – the world's most useless monster.

198 VisitScotland – pushers of kilt-kitsch dependency. Top marks for tartan (e.g. towels, bedcovers, curtains, napkins, carpets, cushions, tea-cups, place- mats, coasters, door-mats, soap, and toilet paper). **Kitsch Sells Scotland – KISS!**

199 The bagpipe is a noble instrument – but not in the hands of street buskers. Intern all such bag-squeezers – use the new terrorism laws.

200 The Scottish Executive discovered a game called golf in Scotland, that tourists play it, and more might be attracted. This became the core of a tourism vision. 'Vision': Government ability to see the end of its nose and declare, at great public expense, that the promised land has been sighted.

201 Our main tourist repellent (apart from weather and VisitScotland) is the midge; if ever exterminated, a plague of tourists could yet descend on us.

202 For tourism not to disappoint visitors or ruin
the environment, it must be discouraged. Happily,
this has long been, and remains, official practice.

Politics

203 Scots will **not** decide if they want independence
because they will **not** decide if they want to be
anything – other, that is, than **Not**-English.

204 The Scots Diaspora does **no**thing for Scotland;
so it's quits historically!

205 Scots broadly welcomed the new Scottish
Parliament. They knew that there wasn't much it
could actually do nowadays – for good or ill. So,
they felt, and feel, no guilt or responsibility for it.
What realists!

206 The new Scottish Parliament is of inestimable, positive, value; it shows Scots what second-raters its members are; so Scots can now give up their historical fantasy that a Parliament might be useful – and get a life.

207 No Parliament ever gained authority with its people without fighting injustice or organising defence. Yes, our MSPs can be relied upon to fight for and defend – their own pay-cheques, allowances, freebies and cronies.

208 The English used native peoples to help colonise their lands. That Empire has long gone, but one colony (England's greatest ever) has survived to this day; Scotland – the world's greatest ever auto-colonialist.

209 The Scots are as capable of governing other
    lands (e.g. England) as they aren't of their own
    (Dr Johnson,

> *'Sir, it is not so much to be lamented that Old
> England is lost, as that the Scotch have found it')*

210 Independent Scotland survived for many
    centuries because it had odd spells of competence
    as a state and occasional good luck; but mainly
    because England had odd spells of the opposite.

211 Scots have droned on about the sovereignty of
    the people since the Declaration of Arbroath 1320.
    This deeply-rooted fancy prevented their making
    parliament effective – either now or long ago. (*For
    as long as 100 of us remain alive we will not submit to
    the power of self awareness.*)

212 Correct the country's name; from Scotland to **Notland**.

213 When Scots lost their Parliament in 1707, they gave up being governed by a small clique of self-servers with a little cash taken from the people. Now it's quite different; there's a huge mob of self-servers spending lots of our cash.

214 The manager of the Scotland football team has a huge following among those who never bother to vote. Boost democracy; make him First Minister.

215 The First Minister should be made to manage
the Scotland football squad. This would teach real
accountability and get rid of duds fast.

216 *'Scots wha hae'*, *'Scotland the Brave'*, *'Flower of
Scotland'*. OK, independence, then – provided we
get one anthem **and** none of these!

217 Twenty-twenty vision – rare among Scots;
unknown among politicians; along with integrity,
it's such a handicap in office, especially at local
level.

218 Local authority officers' clansman-like obeisance to local authority politico-careerists has long undermined urban local authorities. This rot has been observed spreading to the Scottish Executive.

219 The Estates progressed backwards in *'Ane Satyre of the Three Estaitis'*

> *. . . we have gaine sa this mony a yeir.*
> *Howbeit ye think we go undecently,*
> *We think wee gang richt wonder pleasantly. . .*

No change since Sir David Lyndsay's day! Except, politicians have now evolved to have eyes behind their heads: this allows them to see behind, while seeming to look forwards; critically, it protects them from friends in their own party.

220 Call The Scottish 'Executive' a 'Government'; it doesn't/can't execute much; and the name change might nudge it towards what it should be.

221 Scots have never governed themselves happily. And why should it happen soon? Sir David Lyndsay, from 'The Dreme':

> *It is deficill Ryches tyll incres*
> *Quayre Polycie maketh no residence,*
> *And Polycie may never have entres,*
> *Bot quayre that Justyce dois delygence*
> *To puneis quhare thare may be found offence*

222 The merit of the Scottish Parliament; it's **Not** English.

223 If Scotland were **not** part of the English (oops, British) Parliament, it could **not** get by any longer by posing only as **not** English.

224 If politicians read these observations, they'll denounce their negativity. 'Thanks, politicians' – you're a positive inspiration for so many of these observations!

225 Any Scottish politician who denounces these observations confirms the truth of 'Never believe anything till it has been officially denied.'

Scots Symbols

The Scot is symbolised by:

226 The thistle – a prickly thing – first pressed into service a few hundred years ago for fancy-dress purposes (The Order of the Thistle); given fresh encouragement more recently by MacDiarmid – a yet more prickly thing;

227 The rowan tree – an attractive and hardy plant, if overly susceptible to blight known as 'hielanhamitis';

228 The spider (not the lion rampant); not because the spider tries and tries and tries, but because it hardly ever moves, survives on little and – being so small – goes largely unnoticed;

229 Burns's mouse – a pair, wee thing, whose survival is at the mercy of great, uncaring, external, forces;

230 The seal in Celtic myth – the truth of its human origin is obvious when seals gaze ashore; their sorrowful expressions show what a mess they think we've made of things since their time among us;

231 The stag; the would-be establishment's favourite quadruped which, with the sheep and the would-be establishment itself, eats away at Scotland;

232 The Loch Ness Monster; doesn't exist (like the country), yet (like the country) people keep coming to look for it;

233 And, above all, the midge; a tiny, wee thing that lives in damp, barren, places and sucks the blood of any who blunder onto its patch; our chief protector against overpopulation (by resident or tourist).

Stasis

234 The rivers of Scotland run clear and bright towards the open sea. Scotland's public life drifts inland slowly into treacherous swamp.

235 Black Holes absorb energy and emit no light; likewise tradition and self-image for Scotland.

236 It's normal for small countries to imprison their people psychologically; the Scot maintains and guards his prison with abnormal vigour.

International

Everywhere (apart from Scotland or England)

237 Apart from when in Scotland or England, the
Scot is confident and at ease: if **not** in Scotland,
he needn't worry about his social standing; **not** in
England, he needn't worry that he is thought small
and provincial.

238 The Scotsman is loved everywhere for what he is
not – English.

Wales

239 The more the Welsh drink, the better they sing.
The Scot sings badly most times; drink transports
him from harmony to fighting and argument.

Cornwall

240 Cornishmen have taken to wearing the kilt to show they're **Not** English. The Cornishman is the Scotsman's Scotsman.

Ireland

241 Irishmen are caricatured as over-friendly drunks; Scots as steadfast. In the Irish, the vice is considered a virtue; in the Scot, vice versa.

242 The Irish had the Potato Famine, centuries of English rule, and got nothing from Empire. They produced masterpieces of 'English' Literature. Scotland, England's canny collaborator, is too well-off for such nonsense.

243 Scrape up every modern Scottish writer; call Edinburgh an International City of Literature; Dublin is deeply unenvious.

244 The curragh, when it is being made, is like the Scottish Parliament – an upside-down boat; the curragh, however, gets righted later and holds water.

France

245 Scots admire France and French culture because they have difficulty extending the same compliment to England and English culture; anyway as it's culture from far away it has to be good.

246 Scots admire France and French culture; even such a small-minded people as the Scots have to look up to somebody, sometime, for something.

247 De Tocqueville:

> *The French are always looking up to reassure themselves that no one is superior to them; the English are always looking down, to make sure that they are superior to others; in both the fault is the same – pride.*

The Scot does both of these things simultaneously. He also looks about him, lest – in case there just might be someone superior to him – he is not caught off-guard. To the pride of the others he adds fear.

248 Scots show fondness for the 'Auld Alliance' – when the country was under French dynasts. Had Scotland become French, Scots would fondly recall times of peace and harmony between them and English dynasts.

Belgium

249 If we can't name two famous Belgians, imagine
their problem with us!

Germany

250 Scots love Germans because the English don't;
this affection is broadly reciprocated. A fondness
for beer also helps.

America

251 Americans have no past; they believe in their
destiny and in their ability to control it. With
Scots, it's the other way round.

252 The USA's manifest destiny of promoting
democracy and freedom is 200 years old; Scotland
has had the Declaration of Arbroath for 700 years;
each fantasy conceals from these nations the
reality of their State.

253 For an American, to be un-American is the
gravest of offences. In Scotland, to be un-Scottish
is not an offence; it doesn't exist; because it's
inherently impossible for the Scot.

254 The five phases of clan history: Lowland Scots
loathed the clans; they tried to destroy them;
clansmen fled to America; Americans love the
clans; Lowland Scots love the clans.

255 The US two-term limit on Presidents is a
splendid arrangement; it should apply here; above
all to councillors on Local Authorities.

Russia

256 Sokurov (re his film 'Russian Ark'):

> *'Only the creation of the finest art, architecture, music and literature can sustain the idea of a greater humanity, and give it a point of anchorage for the future, a safe haven from the storm.'*

Scotland, adrift, without haven, without anchor.

257 The life-span of Russian males is falling; they drown in rivers when drunk in hot Russian summers. Fortunately for the life-span of the Scottish male, few can swim; anyway, our rivers are Baltic in summer.

Greece

258 The Greek foustanela has 400 pleats – one for each year of Turkish domination. The same for Scotland *vis a vis* England would mean kilts greater than any tailor could stitch or Scotsman's butt support.

259 The modern Greek feels inferiority given the achievements of his ancestors; the Scot feels the same for that and the opposite reason.

260 The Greeks had many Gods; worship of one of them is still popular in Scotland to this day: Dionysus (Bacchus), God of drinking and excess.

261 The Greek drinks as he eats as he talks. The Scot drinks.

Italy

262 Italy – Bella Figura;
  Scotland – shell suits and trainers.

263 Italian diet healthy,
  Scots unhealthy; fish'n chips from Italian
  chippies.

264 *Panem et circusem* – Rome.
  Hot pies and fitba' – Scotland.

265 The gag about Italy's political situation is that
  it's 'grave but not serious'. The Scot has been
  Italianised more than just in the kitchen!

Czechs and Slovaks

266 Which two small EU countries have 5 million
people, a rich capital, and 10% of its people living
in poverty and exclusion? Slovakia and Scotland.
In Slovakia, the 10% are gypsies; here, no such
racist 'excuse' applies.

267 According to the Good Soldier Schweik, every
man should quaff 35 glasses of beer a day. The
Czechs are a small, far away, nation about whom we
know little but from whom we clearly have much
to learn.

268 Surrounded by German-speaking nations, the
Czechs chose to continue to be **Not**-German; they
are the Scots of Central Europe.

Hungarians and Romanians

269 Hungarians and Romanians compete on meanness. They like Aberdonian jokes. Don't tell VisitScotland or they'll compose a 'strategy' to bring more tourists from there – and spend nothing, or millions, on it.

Finland

270 The Finns had high death rates from a fatty diet, poor exercise, etc. They overcame this in part by eating more wild berries. A real Scot would rather be seen dead than eating berries, and will no doubt continue to be so.

271 The Finns encouraged towns to compete against one another on fitness, diet and health; result – success. Scots, as ever, preached; result – failure.

India

272 India has the sacred cow, the white elephant and the untouchables. Scotland has all three in one; Historic Buildings and Ancient Monuments.

China

273 The Scot should give up international sports except one – drinking. And then only with the Chinese. Their genes will guarantee they keel over long before an average Scot. With China's size and wealth, a competitive Scottish drinker would do well all his life – or till his liver packed in, at least.

274 There's evidence of football in China aeons ago!. Great news for Scots! How could we ever be expected to compete in an inscrutable oriental art?

275 Chou en Lai, asked about the effect of the French Revolution, said it was too early to tell. An earlier conclusion on the effectiveness of the Scottish Parliament seems very possible.

276 Alas, even if Scotland disappeared, Auld Lang Zyne (zic) would not – pentatonic harmonies and soupy sentiments appeal too much to the Chinese.

The Jews

277 The Jews, it is said, survived as a response to constant persecution and threat. Where they led, the Scots have taken over.

278 While the Jew has been caricatured as miserly, the Scot has made money and laughs in equal measure out of the same.

Spain

279 Spaniards are mocked for their lazy, laid-back, approach, as expressed in the word 'mañana'; but at least they have a concept for the future.

Portugal

280 The Portuguese think their Fado must be the most bluesy, sad, music in the world. Let them hear a Gaelic psalm – and rejoice!

Spain and Portugal

281 Iberia's paradors and posadas protect, convert and get good returns from built heritage. Scotland's equivalent's in aspic; its economic return marginal.

Bolivia

282 Both in language and gesture, the Aymara look forward to the past and back towards the future. No DNA tests are needed; they must be our ancestors! (Freeze-dried potatoes are their staple diet also.)

Scandinavia

283 Their National Parks have a clear mission – to protect fragile natural beauty. People may enter only on foot. Here, it's different – e.g. ramps **invite** 4x4s onto the shores of the *Bonnie Banks* to launch jet skis.

The Norseman of Old

284 The Norseman fearing the 'straw death' of old age, chose to die young **heroically**. Many young Scots, seeing no prospect of dying heroically, and no point in growing old, choose to die young – **heroinically**.

Norway

285 We like Norwegians because, when they visit us,
   they tell us how mild and agreeable our climate is
   – even in winter,

286 and they're the only people who ever gave us
   territory – Orkney and Shetland.

287 We like the Faroese because we have beaten
   them at football. (*'Bring on Brazil!'*)

Egypt

288 *'If you can't bite the hand, kiss it'*, Egyptians say.
   Scots do both at once with England.

The Zulu Nation

289 The Scots went into battle making a terrific noise. As did Zulus. In the Zulu's case, the noise came from shields and assegais – handy in battle. The Scots used a sheep's bladder – of little comfort to anyone.

The Caribbean

290 Derek Walcott (from *What the Twilight Says*)

> *The Caribbean sensibility is not marinated in the past. It is not exhausted. It is new.*

We knew the Caribbean was different, but . . . !!

Iceland

291 *Under the Glacier,* Halldor Laxness (Translated, Magnus Magnusson, Vintage Books, 2004, ISBN 1- 4000 – 3441- 8)

> *Embi: Hasn't the world been created, then?'*
>
> *Pastor Jon: I thought the creation was still going on. Have you heard that it's been completed?'*

Iceland – a land being formed; Scotland – a land eroding.

The Future

292 Word absent from Scots lexicon.

293 A vague and fearful thing:

> *'But, och! I backward cast my e'e*
> *On prospects drear*
> *An' forward, though I canna see*
> *I guess an fear.'*

294 Unless Global Warming occurs really fast it is to
be expected that, as our bedrock recovers from the
last Ice Age, Scotland will rise up. (The land, that
is!) All the Scot need do meantime (say 10,000
years) is nothing – just like the last 1,000 years.
So, no problem hanging on a bit until England
dips down into the sea and becomes the smaller
part of Great Britain.

295 When the above comes about, the English will
acquire characteristics much like the Scot
historically, and vice versa.

296 When the above comes about, Scots and English
will agree that they do **not** want to be the other.
i.e. as before, only the other way round.

Epilogue

297 *'O wad, some pow'r the giftie gie us*
to see oursels as others see us!'

  Yeah! Now, as then.

298 Forget the past – the hype, the negativity.

299 Think (afresh) – envisage a future.

300 years – the period over which the modern
  Unrealities of Being Scottish have largely
  marinated.